# POPEYE

Bud Sagendorf

**THE ROYAL QUEEN TEST**

**THE DOOMS DAY DOLL**

AF646583

Published by
Westland Books, a division of Nasadiya Technologies Private Limited, in 2025
No. 269/2B, First Floor, 'Irai Arul', Vimalraj Street, Nethaji Nagar, Alapakkam Main Road, Maduravoyal, Chennai 600095

in co-publishing arrangement with
Shakti Comics, The Search House, B-23/C1, Sector 62, Noida, UP



ISBN: 978-93-7197-362-5

10 9 8 7 6 5 4 3 2



Created by E.C. Segar

Written & Illustrated by Bud Sagendorf

Cover Art & Colours: Avishek Biswas

Editor: Vikramaditya



SHAKTI COMICS

# POPEYE

**Popeye** is a tough, fearless sailor-hero whose strength comes not just from his fists, but from his giant heart. He sails through life like a one-man rescue squad, always ready to leap into action when danger sparks. And when the moment truly demands it, he unleashes his legendary spinach surge—an energy boost that turns him into a powerhouse capable of lifting ships, stopping storms, or knocking out any villain who threatens peace. No matter how rough the waves get, Popeye meets every challenge with courage, loyalty, and a never-give-up spirit that makes him feel like a superhero of the seas.

Within his world, Popeye is surrounded by a cast as colorful and lively as any hero team. **Olive Oyl** is the fearless, sharp-witted partner who supports his battles and pushes him to be his best. She may look delicate, but she's brave, clever, and often the heart of Popeye's missions. **Wimpy** brings lighthearted mischief—a friendly companion whose love for hamburgers leads the crew into funny side quests and surprising solutions. And then there's **King Blozo**, the good-natured ruler whose kingdom often teeters on chaos. Whenever danger threatens his land, Blozo turns to Popeye, trusting the sailor's strength and sense of justice to set things right.

Together, they form the core of Popeye's world—friends, allies, and sometimes accidental troublemakers—who shape his adventures and give him reasons to keep fighting. With Olive's courage, Wimpy's humor, and Blozo's trust, Popeye becomes more than a sailor; he becomes a hero who keeps his world safe, strong, and full of heart.

---

# THE ROYAL QUEEN TEST

YOUR MAJESTY, I BELIEVE I CAN HELP YOU!
I NEED HELP TO FIND A WIFE!
YOU HAVE BEEN GOING ABOUT IT IN THE WRONG WAY!
YOU NEED TO HIRE AN ADVERTISING MAN!
12-1
©1999 King Features Syndicate, Inc. World rights reserved.
SHALL WE DISCUSS DETAILS OVER A FEW HAMBURGERS?
BUD SAGENDORF

I AM ADVERTISING IN ALL THE PAPERS FOR A WIFE FOR KING BLOZO!
HM!
12-2
BLOW ME DOWN!? YA DIDN'T RUN A PICTURE OF HIM!?
CURSES, SIR!
I AM **NOT** STUPID..... I ONLY SHOWED PICTURES OF HIS PALACE AND CROWN!
'AT'S GOOD!
BUD SAGENDORF
©1999 King Features Syndicate, Inc. World rights reserved.

AHOY, WIMPY... WHAT'CHA BUILDIN'?
?
BANG!
BANG!
BANG!
12-3
A QUEEN TEST, OL' PAL!
THE APPLICANTS FOR BLOZO'S WIFE HAVE TO WALK THROUGH IT!
ROYAL QUEEN TEST
BUD SAGENDORF
©1999 King Features Syndicate, Inc. World rights reserved.

HOW'S THE QUALIFYIN' CUTOUT WORKIN'?
THE IDEA IS FINE-
ROYAL QUEEN TEST
?
12-4
-BUT THE ONLY ONE TO MAKE IT THROUGH IS A DOG!
TEST
BUD SAGENDORF
©1999 King Features Syndicate, Inc. World rights reserved.

WE'VE HAD SIX HUNDRED APPLICANTS, BUT NONE FIT THE QUEEN CUTOUT!
ROYAL QUEEN TEST
© 1999 King Features Syndicate, Inc. World rights reserved.
I FEAR OUR SEARCH FOR A QUEEN IS HOPELESS!
ROYAL QUEEN TEST
HM?
?
12/6
MY DREAM SAID THAT I WAS GOING TO MARRY A KING!
?
!
12-7
©1999 King Features Syndicate, Inc. World rights reserved.
FATE HAS DECREED I WILL FIT THROUGH THE QUEEN CUTOUT!
HELP!
?
ROYAL QUEEN TEST
HELP!
ROYAL QUEEN TEST
CRAZY DAME TRIED TO FIT THROUGH THE QUEEN CUTOUT!
!
!
PUSH ME THROUGH! I WANT TO BE QUEEN!
GRAB HOLD, WIMPY..... WE HASTA GIT HER UNSTUCK!
© 1999 King Features Syndicate, Inc. World rights reserved.
12-8
I YAM ASHAMED OF YA!
YA KNOWED YA COULDN'T FIT THROUGH THE QUEEN CUTOUT!
MY DREAM SAID I'D BE A QUEEN! DREAMS DON'T LIE!
HM? PERHAPS I DIDN'T TRY HARD ENOUGH!
?
I KNOW I WAS MEANT TO BE A QUEEN!
12-9
© 1999 King Features Syndicate, Inc. World rights reserved.

I KNOW I'LL FIT THROUGH THE QUEEN-TEST CUTOUT!
I JUST DIDN'T TRY HARD ENOUGH!
ROYAL QUEEN TEST
12-10
HERE I COME, YOUR MAJESTY!
THIS TIME I'LL FIT THROUGH!
© 1999 King Features Syndicate, Inc. World rights reserved.
HERE COMES THE QUEEN!
12-11
© 1999 King Features Syndicate, Inc. World rights reserved.
I MADE IT!!
ROYAL QUEEN TEST
?
?
YOUR MAJESTY, I HAVE FOUND YOUR FUTURE QUEEN!
I HOPE SHE IS BEAUTIFUL!
12-13
BEAUTY IS IN THE EYE OF THE BEHOLDER! POPEYE THINKS SHE IS LOVELY!
?
POPEYE? HM? HE'S NOT MUCH OF A JUDGE OF WOMEN!
© 1999 King Features Syndicate, Inc. World rights reserved.
I CAN'T WAIT TO MEET MY BEAUTIFUL BRIDE!
-ER--
?
-ABOUT THAT-- THERE IS A SLIGHT PROBLEM!
THE YOUNG LADY WANTS TO MEET YOU AND YOUR COUNTRY AT THE SAME TIME....SHE WILL JOIN YOU IN SPINACHOVIA!
I'LL GO HOME AND PREPARE A ROYAL WELCOME!
12-14
© 1999 King Features Syndicate, Inc. World rights reserved.

WHY DID YA SEND BLOZO HOME B'FORE HE MET HIS BRIDE ?
IT WAS NECESSARY!
I DIDN'T WANT A REJECTION OF HER BEFORE I GOT PAID!
YOU KNOW HOW HE FEELS ABOUT MISS OYL!
HERE I AM!! WHERE IS MY KING?
12-15
KING BLOZO HAS RETURNED TO SPINACHOVIA!
HUH?
HE WANTS TO PLAN A ROYAL RECEPTION FOR HIS NEW QUEEN!
HOW SWEET! HOW THOUGHTFUL! HE WANTS TO SHOW ME OFF TO HIS PEOPLE!
BLOW ME DOWN! YA CAN'T DO IT, OLIVE! YOU IS ME SWEETIE, AN' B'SIDES, OL' BLOZO CAN'T STAN' YA!
12/16
YOU CAN'T STOP ME FROM BECOMING KING BLOZO'S WIFE!
BUT, OLIVE..
12-17
WHAT ABOUT ME?
OH, YOU.... YOU ALWAYS HAVE YOUR SPINACH!
GOOD HEAVENS!?! WHAT AM I ABOUT TO DO?
12-18
I AM ABOUT TO MARRY A KING--
TEE-HEE!
-AND TOSS ASIDE THE MOST WONDERFUL SAILOR MAN IN THE WORLD!
WOE!
OH, HORROR!
BUD SAGENDORF
©1999 King Features Syndicate, Inc. World rights reserved.

KING BLOZO WANTS TO KNOW WHEN HIS BRIDE IS COMING TO SPINACHOVIA!
I DON'T KNOW!
12/20
©1999 King Features Syndicate, Inc. World rights reserved.
WHAT KIND OF A DUMB SAILOR ARE YOU?
OLIVE IS YOUR ONE AND ONLY SWEETIE, AND YOU DON'T KNOW WHEN SHE'S GOING TO MARRY A KING?
?
?
?
BUD SAGENDORF

IF I MARRY KING BLOZO, POPEYE WILL FIND ANOTHER SWEETIE!
12-21
SAILORS HAVE NO TROUBLE FINDING GIRLS!
©1999 King Features Syndicate, Inc. World rights reserved.
POPEYE!
I LOVE ONLY YOU!
BUD SAGENDORF

WHEN OLIVE DECIDED TO MARRY A KING I GIVED HER UP!
©1999 King Features Syndicate, Inc. World rights reserved.
POPEYE!
?
12-22
SMACK!
I'M BACK!
I DON'T LOVE ANYONE BUT YOU!
WELL, BLOW ME DOWN!
SMACK!
BUD SAGENDORF

I DON'T WANT TO MARRY KING BLOZO!
YA DOESN'T HAVE TO
12-23
©1999 King Features Syndicate, Inc. World rights reserved.
POPEYE, A MESSAGE FROM KING BLOZO!
BUD SAGENDORF
HE'S DECLARED WAR ON YOU!
BLOW ME DOWN!?
BUT POPEYE DIDN'T JILT HIM!
?

WHY WOULD KING BLOZO DECLARE WAR ON ME?
-ER- I HAD TO TELL HIM WHY THE GIRL WOULDN'T MARRY HIM!
?
©1999 King Features Syndicate, Inc. World rights reserved.
I DIDN'T WANT HIM TO BE MAD AT ME!
I TOLD HIM HIS FUTURE BRIDE PREFERRED YOU TO HIM!
!
'AT'S DISGUSTIN'! NO WONDER HE IS MAD AT ME!
!
BUD SAGENDORF
12-24
I HAS NEVER HAD A WHOLE COUNTRY DECLARE WAR ON ME B'FORE!
ARF! ARF! IT COULD BE A REAL GOOD FIGHT!
12-25
AHOY, MISTER GROCERY STORE... I WOULD LIKE TO ORDER A DOZING TRUCKLOADS OF SPINACH!
BIG TRUCKS!
?
BUD SAGENDORF
©1999 King Features Syndicate, Inc. World rights reserved.
I AM GENERAL DE BOOM! I'VE COME FOR KING BLOZO'S BRIDE!
YA CAN'T HAVE HER!
©1999 King Features Syndicate, Inc. World rights reserved.
HM? YOU MUST BE POPEYE!
'AT'S RIGHT!
12/27
IN THE NAME OF KING BLOZO AND SPINACHOVIA, I DECLARE WAR ON YOU!
!
SPLAT!
BUD SAGENDORF
YA MEANS YER WHOLE ARMY IS DECLARIN' WAR ON JUS' ME?
©1999 King Features Syndicate, Inc. World rights reserved.
INDEED WE ARE!
'AT'S STUPID! YA SHOULD PICK ON AN ARMY YA KNOWS YA KIN LICK!
SMACK!
12/28
BUD SAGENDORF

YOU STRUCK THE SPINACHOVIAN GENERAL?
?
I SEZ I DID!
© 1999 King Features Syndicate, Inc. World rights reserved.
THE CRAZY SWAB HAD THE NERVE TO DECLARE WAR ON **ME**!
GENERAL, DID YOU GIVE POPEYE MY MES-SAGE?
YES! AND HE SENT ME BACK AS HIS ANSWER!
?
BUD SAGENDORF
12-29
YOU CAN'T FIGHT A WHOLE ARMY!
PHOOEY! I HAS FIGHTED ELEPHINKS AND OCTOPUSSYS!
12-30
© 1999 King Features Syndicate, Inc. World rights reserved.
BUT YOU'LL BE ONLY **ONE** AGAINST THOUSANDS!
?
YEAH! BUT I ONLY HAS TO LICK **ONE** OF 'EM.. KING BLOZO!
?
?
BUD SAGENDORF
YOU'LL NEVER GET KING BLOZO TO FIGHT YOU!
I KNOWS--
12-31
© 1999 King Features Syndicate, Inc. World rights reserved.
-BUT I HAS A PLAN TO LICK HIM WIT'OUT FIGHTIN'!
HE DON'T KNOW WHO HIS BRIDE IS, SO I YAM SENDING HIM A DAME HE WILL REFUSE TO MARRY!
!
!
!
!
BUD SAGENDORF
WHERE WILL POPEYE FIND A GIRL SO UGLY BLOZO WON'T MARRY HER?
HE SAYS HE KNOWS ONE!
© 1999 King Features Syndicate, Inc. World rights reserved.
AHOY!! INTRODUCING MISS SUE SUDS!
?
1-1
TEE-HEE!
AIN'T I PERTY?
POPEYE?
?
BUD SAGENDORF

DO YOU SEE WHAT I SEE, WIMPY?
-ER-- I THINK SO, MISS OYL!
?
POPEYE!?! IS THAT REALLY YOU?
?
?
BLOW ME DOWN! I SEZ I IS!
OL' BLOZO INSISKS ON A BRIDE, SO I YAM TAKIN' YER PLACE!
I YAM A BLUSHIN' BRIDE!
1-3
BUD SAGENDORF
©2000 King Features Syndicate, Inc. World rights reserved.

OL' KING BLOZO WILL TAKE ONE LOOK AT ME AN' DECIDE HE DON'T WANT TO GIT MARRIED!
?
1-4
BUT WHAT IF HE THINKS YOU ARE BEAUTIFUL?
!
?
BUD SAGENDORF
I WILL BE A NASTY YOUNG THING AN' SMACK HIM SO HARD INTO NEXT WEEK 'AT HE WILL BOUNCE BACK TO LAST TUESDAY!
!
!
©2000 King Features Syndicate, Inc. World rights reserved.

YOU'RE WONDERFUL TAKING MY PLACE AS KING BLOZO'S BRIDE!
IT AIN'T NOTHIN'!
1-5
POPEYE, THERE'S AN ANTIWAR COMMITTEE FROM SPINACHOVIA TO SEE YOU!
?
WE'RE HERE TO SEE THAT A WAR DOESN'T START!
WE WANT TO PLEAD WITH OUR KING'S BRIDE TO GO THROUGH WITH THE MARRIAGE!
?
TEE-HEE!
BUD SAGENDORF
©2000 King Features Syndicate, Inc. World rights reserved.

IF THE GIRL WILL MARRY OUR KING THERE WILL BE NO WAR!
!
1-6
WAR IS HORRIBLE!! I WILL DO IT! I WILL MARRY YER KING!
YIKE!?! IS THAT THING THE BRIDE?
UGH! THERE IS SOMETHING WORSE THAN WAR!
UGH!
?
TELL YER KING HIS BLUSHIN' BRIDE IS ON HIS WAY!
BUD SAGENDORF
©2000 King Features Syndicate, Inc. World rights reserved.

SHE'S UGLY!
UGH!
THAT'S AN UNDER-STATEMENT!
?
?
©2000 King Features Syndicate, Inc. World rights reserved.
A WAR WOULD BE MUCH MORE PLEASANT THAN HAVIN' **THAT** FOR A QUEEN!
1-7
WE'VE SEEN YOUR FUTURE BRIDE!
AS THE ANTIWAR COALITION WE ADVISE YOU TO GO AHEAD WITH THE WAR!
?
?
?
!
BUD SAGENDORF
YOUR FUTURE QUEEN IS IN THE WAITING ROOM!
I CAN'T WAIT TO SEE HER!
©2000 King Features Syndicate, Inc. World rights reserved.
IS SHE BEAUTIFUL?
I BET SHE IS A DREAM DOLL!
I WOULD SUGGEST YOU SIT DOWN TO MEET HER!
?
1-8
BUD SAGENDORF
SEND IN THE BEAUTIFUL GIRL!!
I WANT TO MEET MY FUTURE QUEEN!
©2000 King Features Syndicate, Inc. World rights reserved.
WHAT A GREAT MOMENT IN SPINACHOVIAN HISTORY!
A QUEEN AT LAST!
!
HERE I IS, ME DARLING HUSBING TO BE!
BUD SAGENDORF
1-10
BLOW ME DOWN. WHA' HAPPINGED TO ME FUTURE HUSBING?
HE GOT HIS FIRST LOOK AT YOU!
I TOLD YOU YOU WERE AN **UGLY** DAME!
'AT'S A BLASTID INSULK TO ME FEMININIKYS!
BUD SAGENDORF
1-11
©2000 King Features Syndicate, Inc. World rights reserved.

TAKE IT AWAY! I CAN'T STAND TO LOOK AT IT!
ARF!
©2000 King Features Syndicate, Inc. World rights reserved.
OPEN YOUR EYES, YOUR MAJESTY... I FIXED HER!
ARE YOU SURE?
1-12
BUD SAGENDORF
I PUT A PAPER BAG OVER HER HEAD!
?
UGH! THAT'S NO HELP!! IT'S UGLY **ALL OVER**!
WHY CAN'T I SEE ME FUTURE HUSBING ?
HE CAN'T STAND YOUR UGLY FACE!
©2000 King Features Syndicate, Inc. World rights reserved.
YOUR FACADE UPSETS HIS STOMACH!
!
1-13
'AT'S A BLASTID INSULK! ME FACADE IS AS HEALKTHY AS HIS!
ARMY!
SMACK!
BUD SAGENDORF
YOUR FUTURE BRIDE IS IN PRISON!
PRISON?
©2000 King Features Syndicate, Inc. World rights reserved.
THE UGLY CREATURE STRUCK YOUR GENERAL!
?
?
?
HE INSULKED ME!
1-14
BUD SAGENDORF
YOU BELONG IN PRISON!
I DOESN'T LIKE CAGES!
©2000 King Features Syndicate, Inc. World rights reserved.
YOU STRUCK A GENERAL!
BUD SAGENDORF
SHE DID IT AGAIN!
SPLAT!
SHALL WE DISCUSS OUR WEDDING PLANS, YER MAJESTY?
?
1-15

I'LL CHANGE INTO ME OWN CLOTHES AN' SEE WHAT BLOZO REALLY THINKS OF HIS BRIDE TO BE!
©2000 King Features Syndicate, Inc. World rights reserved.
AHOY, KING BLOZO... I HAS COMED FER YER WEDDING!
BUD SAGENDORF
POPEYE! THANK YOU FOR COMING! YOU CAN HELP ME GET OUT OF THIS HORRIBLE MESS!
?
1-17
YOU DOESN'T LIKE YER BRIDE TA BE?
UGH!
©2000 King Features Syndicate, Inc. World rights reserved.
SHE MAKES THE SEA HAG LOOK LIKE MISS UNIVERSE!
1-18
PERSONALLY, I'D RATHER MARRY MISS OYL!
SHE STRUCK A GENERAL!
ME!
BUD SAGENDORF
I THOUGHT YER PEOPLES WANTED YA TA GIT MARRIED
THEY DO!
©2000 King Features Syndicate, Inc. World rights reserved.
THEY INSIST ON IT!
BUT I'D RATHER BE DEMOTED TO PALACE SWEEPER THAN MARRY A MONSTER!!
EVEN A LOUSY KING HAS SOME PRIDE!
1-19
BUD SAGENDORF
OL' BLOZO DOESN'T KNOW I YAM THE WOMING WHAT HE IS SUSPOSED TO MARRY!
©2000 King Features Syndicate, Inc. World rights reserved.
AHOY, BLOZO... IS YA SURE YER BRIDE TO BE IS AS ARFUL AS YA SEZ?
TWICE SHE STRUCK THE GENERAL!
WE PUT HER IN PRISON AND SHE RIPPED THE DOOR OFF!
RIGHT IN MY HEAD!
SHE'S A BEAST!
1-20
BUD SAGENDORF

YOU DON'T LIKE YER KING'S BRIDE TO BE ?
SHE STRUCK THE GENERAL RIGHT HERE!
© 2000 King Features Syndicate, Inc. World rights reserved.
WHERE ?
RIGHT HERE!
OH! YA MEANS HERE?
POW!
1-21
BUD SAGENDORF

THE SAILOR STRUCK YOUR GENERAL!
POPEYE WILL BE POPEYE!
© 2000 King Features Syndicate, Inc. World rights reserved.
AREN'T YOU GOING TO ORDER ME TO SHOOT HIM?
!
LEAVE MY FRIEND ALONE... IF YOU MUST SHOOT....SHOOT MY UGLY BRIDE TO BE!
OH, GOODY!
BUD SAGENDORF
1-22

YOU SEEMS HAPPY FER A BLASTID GENERAL!
THIS IS A GREAT DAY!
1-24
THE KING IS GOING TO LET ME SHOOT MY CANNON!
© 2000 King Features Syndicate, Inc. World rights reserved.
HE WANTS TO GIT RID OF THE UGLY DAME HE PROMISED TO MARRY!
?
BLOW ME DOWN?
BOOM! BOOM!
HE WANTS ME TO SHOOT HER!
BUD SAGENDORF

YA CAN'T LET YER GENERAL SHOOT YER BRIDE TO BE!
HA!
I DIDN'T PICK HER OUT! YOU AND WIMPY DID!
!
AND I WANT YOU TO KNOW I THINK YOU BOTH HAVE VERY BAD TASTE!
1-25
BUD SAGENDORF
© 2000 King Features Syndicate, Inc. World rights reserved.

PRIVATE, ROLL OUT THE ROYAL CANNON OF SPINACHOVIA!
YES, SIR!
© 2000 King Features Syndicate, Inc. World rights reserved.
I WONDER WHAT IT LOOKS LIKE!
THE ROYAL CANNON, GENERAL!
HM? WHERE DOES THE BOOM-BOOM GO IN?
?
BUD SAGENDORF
1-26
GOOD HEAVENS! THE ROYAL CANNON HAS A HOLE IN IT!
CURSES!
PRIVATE! WHAT IS A HOLE DOING IN THE END OF THE KING'S CANNON?
THAT'S WHERE THE ROYAL BOOM COMES OUT, GENERAL!
OH!
BUD SAGENDORF
1-27
© 2000 King Features Syndicate, Inc. World rights reserved.
THE GENERAL HAS ORDERS TO SHOOT THE KING'S BRIDE TO BE! ARF! ARF! THEY DON'T KNOW I YAM HER!
© 2000 King Features Syndicate, Inc. World rights reserved.
AHOY, GENERAL, IT'S A NICE DAY FOR A WEDDING, AIN'T IT?
BAH!
BLOW ME DOWN! WHAT A BIG SHOOTS GUN!
ISN'T IT NICE? THE KING IS GOING TO LET ME SHOOT IT!
LOOK INTO THE BEAUTIFUL HOLE AND SEE HOW SHINY IT IS!
1-28
BUD SAGENDORF
LOOK IN THE NICE HOLE... YOU'LL SEE A CUTE LITTLE BIRDIE!
?
© 2000 King Features Syndicate, Inc. World rights reserved.
PRIVATE! FRONT AND CENTER!
WHERE IS THE TRIGGER TO MAKE THE BOOM-BOOM?
HM?
1-29
BUD SAGENDORF

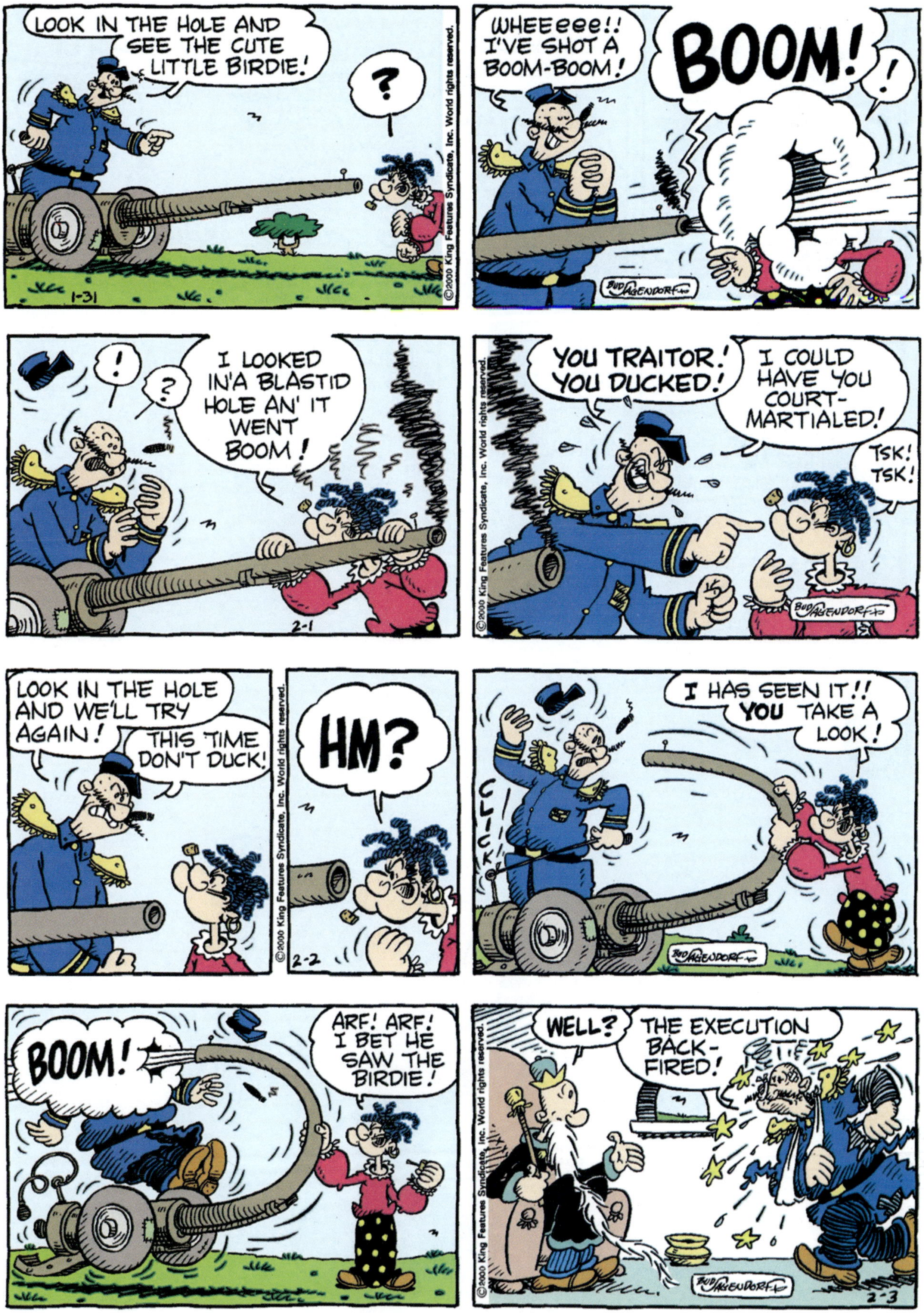
LOOK IN THE HOLE AND SEE THE CUTE LITTLE BIRDIE!
?
1-31
©2000 King Features Syndicate, Inc. World rights reserved.
WHEEeee!! I'VE SHOT A BOOM-BOOM!
BOOM!
!
BUD SAGENDORF
!
?
I LOOKED IN'A BLASTID HOLE AN' IT WENT BOOM!
2-1
YOU TRAITOR! YOU DUCKED!
I COULD HAVE YOU COURT-MARTIALED!
TSK! TSK!
©2000 King Features Syndicate, Inc. World rights reserved.
BUD SAGENDORF
LOOK IN THE HOLE AND WE'LL TRY AGAIN!
THIS TIME DON'T DUCK!
©2000 King Features Syndicate, Inc. World rights reserved.
HM?
2-2
I HAS SEEN IT!! YOU TAKE A LOOK!
CLICK
BUD SAGENDORF
BOOM!
ARF! ARF! I BET HE SAW THE BIRDIE!
WELL?
THE EXECUTION BACK-FIRED!
©2000 King Features Syndicate, Inc. World rights reserved.
BUD SAGENDORF
2-3

POPEYE! HELP!!
I DON'T WANT TO MARRY A BEAST!
©2000 King Features Syndicate, Inc. World rights reserved.
AHOY, YER MAJESTY, DID YA CALL ME?
HELP!
2-4
POPEYE!?! YOU'RE WEARING A DRESS!?
GULP! I FERGOT! I LEFT ORF ME WIG!
NOW HE KNOWS I YAM HIS UGLY BRIDE TO BE!!
BUD SAGENDORF

YOU TOOK MISS OYL'S PLACE SO I WOULDN'T HAVE TO MARRY HER?
'AT'S RIGHT! YER ME FRIEN' AN' SHE IS ME SWEETIE!
©2000 King Features Syndicate, Inc. World rights reserved.
YOU HAVE EARNED THE ROYAL MEDAL OF SPINACHOVIA!
WELL, BLOW ME DOWN!!
I YAM A BLASTID HERO!
I SAVED A ROYAL KING!
-AN' I GOT OLIVE OUT OF ANOTHER OF HER STUPID MESSES!
2-5
BUD SAGENDORF

SPINACH

DOOMSDAY DOLL!
KISS ME, SAILOR BOY!

# POPEYE

STARTING NOW
"The DOOMSDAY DOLL!"
A TALE OF HORROR AND LOVE!!
I HAS HAD AN' OL' SEAMAN'S PREMONITION!
A DISASTER IS PLANNIN' TO HAPPEN TO YOU!!
2-7
WHEEeee!! IT IS LEAP YEAR!!
LET'S SEE WHAT THE WITCHES' HANDBOOK HAS TO SAY!!
"THE YEAR OF THE LEAP IS THE IDEAL TIME TO DEMOLISH, ABOLISH AND PULVERIZE ONE-EYED SALT-WATER SAILORS!"
© King Features Syndicate, Inc. 2000. World rights reserved.
BUD SAGENDORF
PAPPY HAS AN OL' SEAMAN'S PREMONITION ABOUT ME!
DOES HE SEE YOU GETTING MARRIED?
2-8
NOTHIN' AS DISASTROUS AS THAT!
!
?
IT IS MORE LIKE AN EARTHQUAKE.. TYPHOON.. OR THE END OF THE WORLD!
© King Features Syndicate, Inc. 2000. World rights reserved.
BUD SAGENDORF
HA! HA!
YOU DON'T PUT ANY FAITH IN AN OLD SEAMAN'S PREMONITION, DO YOU?
HE'S ME PAPPY!
© King Features Syndicate, Inc. 2000. World rights reserved.
YOUR PAPPY IS A SILLY OLD GOAT!!
!
2-9
I HAS AN OL' SEAMAN'S PREMONITION FER YOU, BIG MOUTH.... IN ONE SECOND YOU IS GO'NER GIT A PUNCH ON'A NOSE!!
PAPPY!! 'AT'S NO WAY TO TALK TO A LADY!
BUD SAGENDORF
YA DOESN'T THINK AN OL' SEAMAN'S PREMONITION IS DEPENDABLE?
OF COURSE NOT!!
© King Features Syndicate, Inc. 2000. World rights reserved.
IF PAPPY BELIEVED DISASTER WAS ABOUT TO STRIKE HE'D DO SOME-THING!
?
!
?
'BYE, SON!! THIS RAT IS LEAVIN' THIS SINKIN' SHIP!
AVAST! MAN THE BOATS!
BUD SAGENDORF
2-10

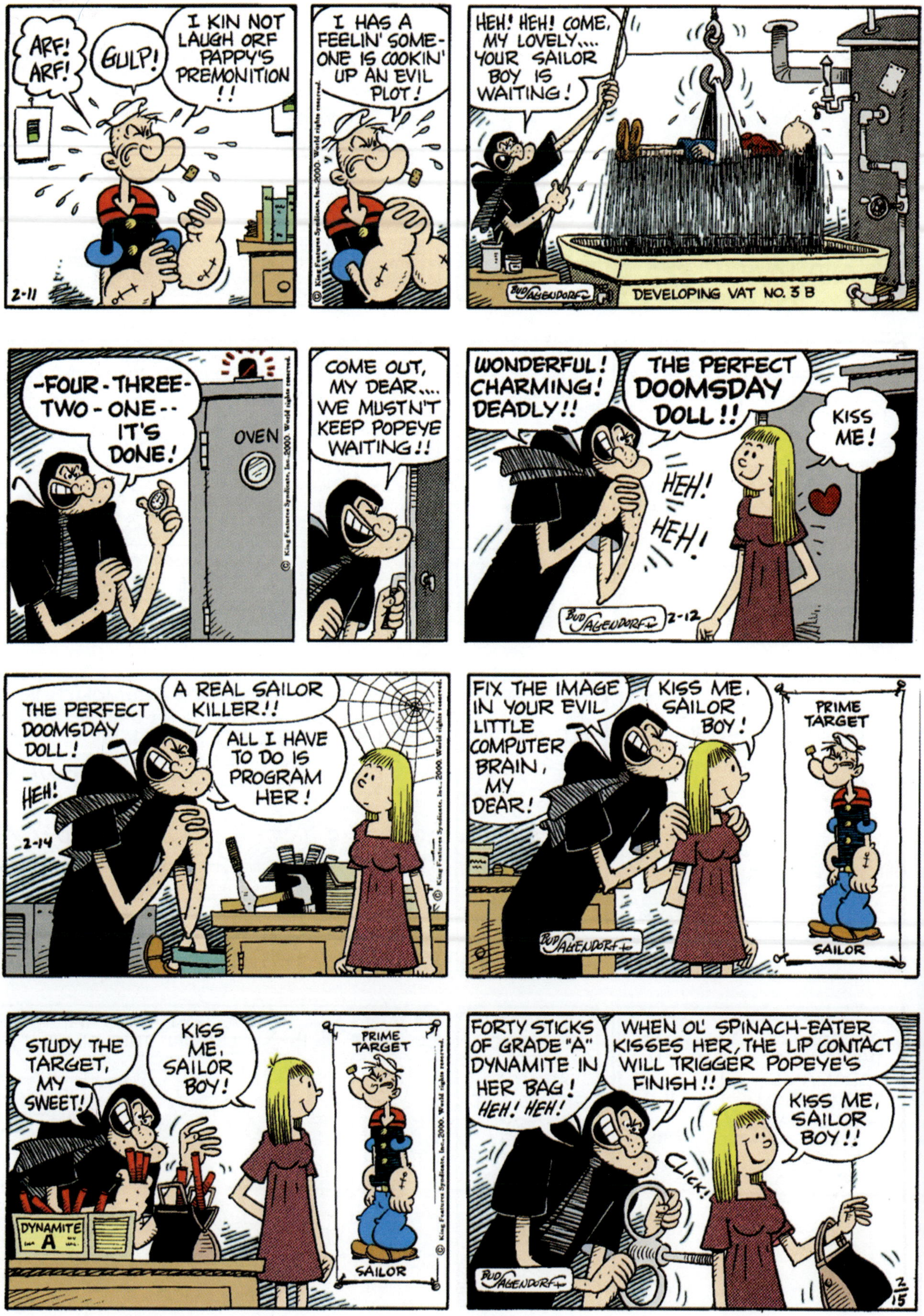
ARF! ARF!
GULP!
I KIN NOT LAUGH ORF PAPPY'S PREMONITION !!
2-11
I HAS A FEELIN' SOME-ONE IS COOKIN' UP AN EVIL PLOT!
© King Features Syndicate, Inc., 2000. World rights reserved.
HEH! HEH! COME, MY LOVELY.... YOUR SAILOR BOY IS WAITING!
BUD SAGENDORF
DEVELOPING VAT NO. 3 B
-FOUR - THREE - TWO - ONE -- IT'S DONE!
OVEN
COME OUT, MY DEAR.... WE MUSTN'T KEEP POPEYE WAITING!!
WONDERFUL! CHARMING! DEADLY!!
THE PERFECT DOOMSDAY DOLL!!
KISS ME!
HEH! HEH!
BUD SAGENDORF 2-12
THE PERFECT DOOMSDAY DOLL!
A REAL SAILOR KILLER!!
ALL I HAVE TO DO IS PROGRAM HER!
HEH!
2-14
FIX THE IMAGE IN YOUR EVIL LITTLE COMPUTER BRAIN, MY DEAR!
KISS ME, SAILOR BOY!
PRIME TARGET
SAILOR
BUD SAGENDORF
STUDY THE TARGET, MY SWEET!
KISS ME, SAILOR BOY!
PRIME TARGET
SAILOR
DYNAMITE A
FORTY STICKS OF GRADE "A" DYNAMITE IN HER BAG! HEH! HEH!
WHEN OL' SPINACH-EATER KISSES HER, THE LIP CONTACT WILL TRIGGER POPEYE'S FINISH!!
KISS ME, SAILOR BOY!!
CLICK!
BUD SAGENDORF
2 15

ARE YOU STILL WORRIED?
I SEZ I IS! I KNOWS A DISASTER IS AFTER ME!
I KIN FEEL IT GITTING CLOSER AN' CLOSER!
THERE'S THE TARGET, DOOMSDAY DOLL!
KISS ME, SAILOR BOY!
GO!
SIC 'EM!
CHARGE!
2-16
DO YOU KNOW HER?
I HAS NEVER SEED HER B'FORE IN ME LIFE!
I AM DEE-DEE THE DOOMSDAY DOLL!
2-17
?
?
KISS ME, SAILOR BOY!!
HEH! HEH!
WHAT DID YOU SAY?
I AM DEE-DEE THE DOOMSDAY DOLL!
2/18
!
KISS ME, SAILOR BOY!
?
?
THAT'S WHAT I THOUGHT YOU SAID!
BONK!
?
!
CURSES! I FORGOT OLIVE WOULD BE JEALOUS OF A STRANGER!
I SHOULD HAVE KNOWN SHE WOULDN'T LET YOU KISS POPEYE!!
I AM DEE-DEE THE DOOMSDAY DOLL!
KISS ME, SAILOR BOY!
I AM--
CLICK!
CLANK!
I AM DEE-DEE.. KISS ME, SAILOR BOY!!
KISS!
OH, WELL.. BACK TO THE DRAWING BOARD!
2-19

I KIN FEEL ME DISASTER GITTIN' CLOSER!
'AT CRAZY GIRL WANTIN' TO KISS ME WAS A BAD OMEN!!
BAH!
IT WAS A VERY BAD OMEN, BUT IT WASN'T FOR YOU!
© King Features Syndicate, Inc., 2000. World rights reserved.
ARF! ARF!! YA IS RIGHT!! IT WEREN'T ME BAD OMEN, WERE IT?
ARF!
TEE-HEE! I DID SMASH HER RATHER GOOD!!
IMAGINE A STRANGER WANTING MY SAILOR BOY TO KISS HER!
2-21
BUD SAGENDORF
THERE HAS TO BE A WAY TO MAKE POPEYE KISS THE DOOMSDAY DOLL!
DEE-DEE!
KISS ME, SAILOR BOY!
© King Features Syndicate, Inc., 2000. World rights reserved.
SHUD-UP! I'M TRYING TO THINK EVIL THINKS!
I'LL HAVE TO RESORT TO NASTY TRICKERY..... I'LL MAKE OLIVE LET POPEYE KISS HER!
BLUB--
MUMBLE!
?
TICK-TOCK!
CLANK!
EVIL DOINGS HOW TO-
2/22
BUD SAGENDORF
2-22
SHE'LL HAVE TO BE PROPERLY INTRODUCED TO POPEYE!
DEE-DEE!
KISS ME!
© King Features Syndicate, Inc., 2000. World rights reserved.
WHAT I NEED IS THE HELP OF SOME UNSCRUPULOUS PERSON!
HM?
♫ HELLO, WIMPY... THIS IS HAGGY... I HAVE A HAMBURGER ON THE FIRE! ♫
I AM DEE-DEE THE DOOMSDAY DOLL!
KISS ME, SAILOR BOY!
CLICK!
TICK-TOCK
HEH!
HEH!
2-23
BUD SAGENDORF
GREETINGS! HAGGY INVITED ME FOR HAMBURGERS!
I AM DEE-DEE THE DOOMSDAY DOLL!
© King Features Syndicate, Inc., 2000. World rights reserved.
2-24
!
KISS ME, SAILOR BOY!
AH! WELLINGTON, YOU HAVE ARRIVED!
DO YOU HAVE A SAILOR SUIT I CAN BORROW?
I AM DEE-DEE THE DOOMSDAY DOLL!
KISS ME-
TICK-TOCK!
BUD SAGENDORF

INTRODUCE ME TO THE YOUNG LADY!
SHE IS YOUR COUNTRY COUSIN!
HEH! HEH!
2 25
© King Features Syndicate, Inc., 2000. World rights reserved.
SHE IS?
KISS ME, SAILOR BOY!
I DIDN'T KNOW I HAD A LOVELY YOUNG COUSIN!
I AM DEE-DEE!
?
YOU DIDN'T! I JUST MADE HER.... YOU ARE GOING TO HELP HER KILL YOUR PAL POPEYE!
?
BUD SAGENDORF
I WILL NOT HELP YOU KILL POPEYE!
CURSES! I NEED HIS HELP, AND HE'S GETTING SENTIMEN-TAL!
BAH!
2-26
BUD SAGENDORF
I WAS HOPING I WOULDN'T HAVE TO HYPNOTIZE HIM!!
KEEP YOUR EYES ON THE NICE HAMBURGER!
YOUR EYES ARE GETTING HEAVY!!
HO-HUM!
SLEEP!
?
© King Features Syndicate, Inc., 2000. World rights reserved.
WATCH THE SWINGING HAMBURGER!
YOU ARE IN MY POWER.... YOU WILL THINK AND DO AS I WISH!
DO AS YOU WISH!
SLEEP!
SLEEP!
HO-HUM!
THE DOOMSDAY DOLL IS YOUR OWN SWEET COUNTRY COUSIN!
KISS ME, SAILOR BOY!
SHE IS MY COUNTRY COUSIN! SHE WILL DESTROY MY BEST FRIEND!
TICK-TOCK!
2-28
BUD SAGENDORF
© King Features Syndicate, Inc., 2000. World rights reserved.
TESTING! ONE-TWO-THREE--
WHO IS THE YOUNG LADY?
SHE IS MY SWEET COUNTRY COUSIN! SHE WILL DESTROY MY BEST FRIEND!
2 29
TICK
BUD SAGENDORF
HEH! HEH! HE IS COMPLETELY HYPNOTIZED!
HE WILL CARRY OUT MY EVIL PLOT!!
COME, DEE-DEE... I'LL INTRODUCE YOU TO POPEYE
KISS ME, SAILOR BOY!
HEH!
TICK-TOCK!
CLICK!
© King Features Syndicate, Inc., 2000. World rights reserved.

HEH! HEH! WIMPY IS ON HIS WAY TO INTRODUCE DEE-DEE TO POPEYE!
THE STUPID SAILOR WILL KISS HER AND "BOOM"! NO MORE POPEYE!
3-1
AWK!?! WHA-TH---? BLAST!
CURSES! THE DOOMSDAY DOLL FORGOT HER BAG OF DYNAMITE!
HER KISSES ARE PUNCHLESS WITHOUT THE BOOM-BOOM!
© King Features Syndicate, Inc., 2000. World rights reserved.
BUD SAGENDORF

YOU FORGOT YOUR BAG!
I AM DEE-DEE THE DOOMSDAY DOLL!
KISS ME!
TICK-TOCK!
© King Features Syndicate, Inc., 2000. World rights reserved.
DOES MY COUNTRY COUSIN NEED A BAG TO MEET POPEYE?
OF COURSE SHE DOES! WHEN POPEYE KISSES HER THE BAG OF DYNAMITE WILL GO BOOM!
IF YOU HADN'T HYPNOTIZED ME I WOULD NEVER PERMIT SUCH AN EVIL ROMANCE!
KISS ME, SAILOR BOY!
3-2
BUD SAGENDORF

GR-R-R!
BLOW ME DOWN!?! HERE COMES WIMPY WIT' 'AT STRANGE GIRL!
3-3
OL' FRIEND, I WOULD LIKE YOU TO MEET MY COUNTRY COUSIN!
I AM DEE-DEE THE DOOMSDAY DOLL!! KISS ME, SAILOR BOY!
YA KIN NOT SMACK HER! SHE IS A FRIEN' OF THE FAMILY!
I'LL KILL HER!
© King Features Syndicate, Inc., 2000. World rights reserved.
BUD SAGENDORF

ARE YOU SURE SHE IS YOUR COUSIN, WIMPY?
INDEED SHE IS... FRESH FROM THE COUNTRY!
I AM DEE-DEE THE DOOMSDAY DOLL!
GR-R-
!
3-4
ISN'T IT NICE... MY COUSIN LIKES MY BEST FRIEND!
KISS ME, SAILOR BOY!!
I KIN NOT DO IT... ME LIPS IS SAVED FER THE WOMING I LOVES!!
GR-R-
© King Features Syndicate, Inc., 2000. World rights reserved.
BUD SAGENDORF

KISS ME, SAILOR BOY!
GR-R!
HEH! HEH! WIMPY HAS FORMALLY INTRODUCED THE DOOMSDAY DOLL TO POPEYE!
MY KILLER BOMB HAS BEEN PLANTED!
3-6
KISS ME, SAILOR BOY!
A SWEET YOUNG THIN' SHOULDN'T ASK MENS TO KISS HER!
IT AIN'T DIGMAFIED ACTIONS FER A COUNTRY COUSIN!
TICK-TOCK!
CURSES! HAS HE FORGOTTEN HE'S A SAILOR?
BUD SAGENDORF
KISS ME, SAILOR BOY!
I DOES NOT KISS NO DAMES BUT THE WOMING I LOVES!
HA!
CURSES! THE OLD HAG ISN'T GOING TO LIKE THIS!
3-7
YOU LET HIM GET AWAY WITHOUT KISSING THE DOOMSDAY DOLL!
I GUESS HE DOESN'T BELIEVE IN KISSIN' COUSINS!
KISS ME, SAILOR BOY!
BUD SAGENDORF
POPEYE ONLY LIKES TO SMOOCH WITH MISS OYL!
HE HAS TO KISS THE DOOMSDAY DOLL TO MAKE THE BOMB GO OFF!
PERHAPS IF YOU WORKED UPON HIS SYMPATHIES!
HM? A SPLENDID IDEA... NO SAILOR CAN RESIST A LADY'S TEARS!
I'LL LOAD HER WITH ENOUGH TEARS TO MAKE POPEYE FORGET A THOUSAND OLIVES!
SALT WATER
KISS ME!
3-8
BUD SAGENDORF
I'M PROUD OF YOU FOR NOT KISSING WIMPY'S COUNTRY COUSIN!
ME LIPS IS ONLY FER YOU!
3-9
POPEYE! POPEYE!
COME AT ONCE!! MY COUNTRY COUSIN HAS TO TALK TO YOU!!
I BET SHE WANTS TO APOLOGIZE!
DON'T GO!! IT'S A TRICK!
BUD SAGENDORF

MY COUNTRY COUSIN HAS TO TALK TO YOU!
I BET SHE WANTS TO APOLOGIZE TO ME!
SHE REALIZES IT IS WRONG FER GIRLS TO ASK SAILORS TO KISS HER!
KISS ME OR I'LL CRY!!
POPEYE IS UNFAIR TO COUNTRY COUSINS!
GR-R-R!
BAH!
3/10
KISS ME, SAILOR BOY, OR I'LL CRY!!
PLEASE DON'T CRY... US SAILORS CAN'T STAND TO SEE DAMES CRY!!
HEH! HEH!
3/11
NOW I'LL ACTIVATE DEE-DEE'S TEAR DUCTS AND HIT POPEYE IN HIS SAILOR HEART!
CONTROL
BLOW ME DOWN!?!
GOOD HEAVENS?
CLICK!
KISS ME OR I'LL CRY!
BLOW ME DOWN!?! I HAS NEVER SEED SUCH TEARS B'FORE!
CURSES!! I CAN'T TURN OFF HER TEAR DUCTS!
THE CONTROL IS STUCK!
IT'S GETTING DAMP... I THINK YOU SHOULD KISS HER!
POOR LI'L COUNTRY COUSIN!
HELP! I'LL DROWN!
3-13
SHE'S STOPPED CRYING, OL' PAL!
I AM DEE-DEE THE DOOMSDAY DOLL...KISS ME, SAILOR BOY!
CURSES! SHE CRIED A MILLION GALLONS AND POPEYE DIDN'T KISS HER!
LET'S GET OUT OF THIS PUDDLE!
3-14
POPEYE HAS TO KISS HER TO SET OFF THE DYNAMITE IN HER BAG!
P-SSS-T, WELLINGTON....TELL MISS OYL YOU'LL GIVE HER THIS FIVE THOUSAND IF SHE WILL LET POPEYE KISS THE DOOMSDAY DOLL!!

MAY I SPEAK TO YOU ?
OF COURSE, WIMPY!
I'LL GIVE YOU FIVE THOUSAND IF YOU'LL GET POPEYE TO KISS MY COUNTRY COUSIN!
!
HOW DARE YOU SUGGEST SUCH A THING?
DO I LOOK LIKE THE GREEDY TYPE THAT WOULD SELL MY LOVE'S KISSES?
?
!
I AM DEE-DEE THE DOOMSDAY DOLL...KISS ME, SAILOR BOY!
ME LIPS B'LONGS TO OLIVE!
POPEYE, DEAR.... GIVE THE SWEET YOUNG THING A KISS!
?
OLIVE!?! WHA'S THE IDEA?
KISS ME, SAILOR BOY!
WHY DOES YA WANT ME TO DO SUCH A HORRIBLE THING?
-ER- TEE-HEE..... I HAVE FIVE THOUSAND REASONS WHY I WANT YOU TO KISS HER!
ONE KISS WON'T HURT ME MUCH!!
KISS ME, SAILOR BOY!
I WILL TRY ON ACCOUNT OF OLIVE WANTS ME TO!
STOP!
TIE ME TO THIS TREE SO I WON'T KILL THEM WHEN THEY KISS!!
?
?
WHEEeee!! POPEYE IS ABOUT TO KISS THE DOOMSDAY DOLL! HEH! HEH!!
IT WILL BE HIS LAST KISS!
IS YA READY?
KISS ME, SAILOR BOY!
YA AIN'T MAKIN' IT ANY EASIER, OLIVE!
IT'LL BE OVER IN A MINUTE, MISS OYL!
I CAN'T STAND IT!! I'LL KILL THEM BOTH!

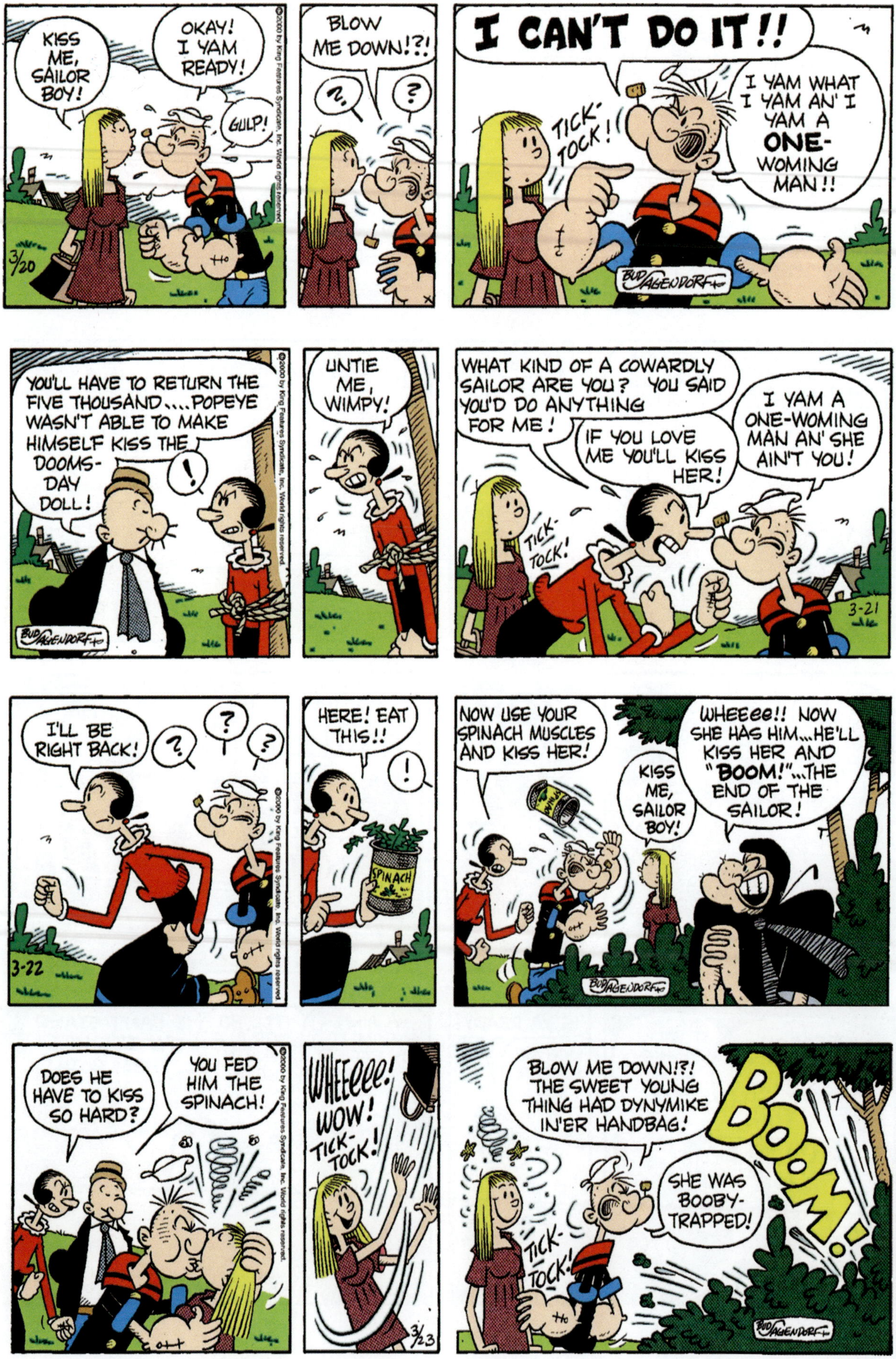
KISS ME, SAILOR BOY!
OKAY! I YAM READY!
GULP!
©2000 by King Features Syndicate, Inc. World rights reserved
3/20
BLOW ME DOWN!?!
?
?
I CAN'T DO IT!!
TICK-TOCK!
I YAM WHAT I YAM AN' I YAM A **ONE-**WOMING MAN!!
BUD SAGENDORF
YOU'LL HAVE TO RETURN THE FIVE THOUSAND....POPEYE WASN'T ABLE TO MAKE HIMSELF KISS THE DOOMS-DAY DOLL!
!
©2000 by King Features Syndicate, Inc. World rights reserved
BUD SAGENDORF
UNTIE ME, WIMPY!
WHAT KIND OF A COWARDLY SAILOR ARE YOU? YOU SAID YOU'D DO ANYTHING FOR ME!
IF YOU LOVE ME YOU'LL KISS HER!
I YAM A ONE-WOMING MAN AN' SHE AIN'T YOU!
TICK-TOCK!
3-21
I'LL BE RIGHT BACK!
?
?
?
©2000 by King Features Syndicate, Inc. World rights reserved
3-22
HERE! EAT THIS!!
!
SPINACH
NOW USE YOUR SPINACH MUSCLES AND KISS HER!
KISS ME, SAILOR BOY!
WHEEee!! NOW SHE HAS HIM...HE'LL KISS HER AND "**BOOM!**"...THE END OF THE SAILOR!
BUD SAGENDORF
DOES HE HAVE TO KISS SO HARD?
YOU FED HIM THE SPINACH!
©2000 by King Features Syndicate, Inc. World rights reserved.
WHEEeee! WOW! TICK-TOCK!
3/23
BLOW ME DOWN!?! THE SWEET YOUNG THING HAD DYNYMIKE IN'ER HANDBAG!
SHE WAS BOOBY-TRAPPED!
TICK-TOCK!
BOOM!
BUD SAGENDORF

3/24
HER BAG EXPLODED WHEN YOU KISSED HER!
I YAM GLAD SHE TOSSED IT IN THOSE BUSHES!
BLAST! # !!
BAH!!
CURSE!
BUD SAGENDORF
IT'S THE SEA HAG!
?
BLAST YOU, POPEYE! I'M TAKING MY DOLL HOME!!
NEXT TIME YOU WON'T BE SO LUCKY!
KISS ME, SAILOR BOY!
TICK-TOCK!
©2000 by King Features Syndicate, Inc. World rights reserved.

I WAS HYPNOTIZED BY THE OLD SEA HAG!
AN' IT WAS JUS' A MECHANICAL DOLL WHAT I KISSED!!
3/25
THE DOOMSDAY DOLL WAS A BOOBY-TRAP SET TO KILL YOU!
©2000 by King Features Syndicate, Inc. World rights reserved.
YOUR SPINACH-KISS WAS TOO MUCH FOR HER COMPUTER BRAIN.....SHE WENT OUT OF CONTROL!!
SOMEDAY THA' OL' SEA HAG IS GO'NER MAKE ME REAL MAD!
WHEN HE KISSES ME THERE'S NO BIG BOOM!?!
?
?
BUD SAGENDORF

# POPEYE

Elzie Crisler Segar was the creative force who launched Popeye into the world. Growing up in the small river town of Chester, Illinois, Segar worked many odd jobs—painting houses, playing drums for local shows, even running the film projector at his neighborhood theater. But deep down, he dreamed of becoming an artist. As a teenager, he trained late into the night through a mail-in cartooning course, determined to turn his passion into his life's calling.

His journey took him to Chicago, where he met well-known cartoonist Richard Felton Outcault, who encouraged him and helped him land his first professional work. Segar created several early strips and eventually moved to New York to join King Features Syndicate. There, he began drawing a strip called **Thimble Theatre**—which originally starred Olive Oyl, her family, and Ham Gravy. The strip slowly grew in popularity, gaining a Sunday edition and developing longer, more adventurous storylines.

Everything changed in 1929, when Segar introduced a tough, fearless sailor named Popeye. Readers immediately connected with the spinach-powered hero, and demand for Popeye skyrocketed. Within just a few years, Popeye transformed the entire strip into a national phenomenon—bringing animated films, merchandise, and a whole expanding cast of unforgettable characters like Wimpy, Poopdeck Pappy, Alice the Goon, and Eugene the Jeep. By the time of Segar's passing in 1938, Popeye had become one of the most beloved heroes in American pop culture.

Segar signed his work as "Segar" or sometimes with a little cigar drawing—because people often pronounced his name "SEE-gar." After his death, his legacy continued through other artists, most notably Bud Sagendorf, who had been his assistant and went on to carry Popeye's adventures forward for decades. Thanks to Segar's imagination and determination, Popeye's world grew into a bright, heroic universe that continues to inspire readers of all ages.